So You Want To Be A Nurse?

Success Strategies for Nursing Students

By

Robert L. Anders, Dr.PH. CS, CNAA, ANEF, FAAN
LTC (Ret) USA

Dedication

This book is dedicated to all potential and current nursing students. The calling to be a nurse is life transforming, not only for yourself, your loved ones but also for those countless lives for which your caring touch will make a difference.

Author's Note

This eBook originated from my experience as a nurse educator and academic administrator for a variety of nursing programs. I started my nursing career as a second lieutenant in the Army caring for those serving our country in the Vietnam War. My career has included working as a staff nurse, a charge nurse, a nurse manager, a chief nursing officer to a nurse educator progressing from instructor, professor emeritus to vice president of nursing. I want to share with you some thoughts and suggestions in how your journey as a nursing student may somehow be hopefully impacted by my "words of wisdom".

Students have limited resources to assist them in understanding what to expect in their journey to become a nurse. This short eBook is designed to provide a general overview to aid students, their families and/or significant others in gaining a better understanding of nursing schools. I offer my thoughts to you for whatever assistance they may provide you.

Chapter 1 discusses some of the considerations and options involved in the decision to become a nurse and if it is your calling. Chapter 2 discusses various issues and consideration as you get ready for nursing school. Information is provided to aid you in deciding which nursing program is right for you including information on regulatory issues and the licensing examination. Admission requirements, tuition and fees, and financial aid options are also discussed. Chapter 3 discusses what you are going to need once you start nursing school. Understanding the curriculum is described on Chapter 5. Chapter 6 is the heart of the eBook providing you detailed information and guidance in how to be successful in mastering the nursing content.   In Chapter 7, clinical expectations and competencies are covered while in Chapter 8, program evaluation is discussed. Chapter 9 describes a variety of extra curriculum activities that are available to students.

These are my words, and I have listed resources which aided me in compiling this text. I am solely responsible for its content and every effort has been made to insure accuracy.

Robert Anders

CHAPTER ONE

Starting Your Journey to Nursing School

Choosing a career can be difficult for many people today, and one of the reasons that it is so challenging is the fact that they are looking only at certain facets of the career, such as money. If you were to choose a career based solely on the earning potential that it offers, there is every chance that you will be in a job that you dislike. When you are choosing your field, find something about which you have an interest or passion, and that will help make your career far more enjoyable for you.

A career in nursing could actually be something that would be perfect for many out there looking for a challenge and a career that can pay well and offer many rewards. Nurses are intelligent, nimble minded, and able to work in many capacities in the healthcare field, from clinics, community settings, hospitals and schools. Nurses are most frequently employed in hospital settings from intensive care units, emergency rooms, maternity, surgery, to medical and surgical units.

The Calling to Become a Nurse

For quite a few who are working as nurses today, there was something of a calling to work in the field. Some people have the will and the drive to become a nurse because they want so badly to be able to help others who are in need. Others love the challenge and the science the field offers. They all genuinely care about the wellbeing of strangers, no matter which area of nursing they enter through.

For some, this desire to become a nurse starts at an early age and just never lets up. Others do not feel the call to get a degree and work as a nurse until they are a bit older and exploring different career options.

When you start to explore all of the different options and possibilities that the profession of nursing offers, you will see that there are quite a few different choices when it comes to your career path. Whether you want to work directly with patients in a clinic, in a nursing unit, in the community, you have some great opportunities available.

Nursing is a more than a scientific profession. It is a compassionate art form that involves knowing how to work with patients who are in different states of health, mind or agitation, and how to complete countless nursing procedures. It is entails understanding how to deal with the stresses of patients, coworkers, and physicians at the same time. This is definitely an art form!

How Do Nurses Change Lives?

Anyone who has ever had to go to a clinic, stay in a hospital, or visited someone in a hospital or a nursing home knows what a difference a good nurse can make. Hospitals are frightening places for many people. They could have loved ones that are sick, they could be going in for a procedure, or they could be there for rehabilitation. No matter the reason someone is there, it's easy to see why hospitals have such a bad reputation. They are a place where some scary and sad things may well happen.

The nurses who work in these clinics and hospitals are the beacons of light that are able to brighten the days of those around them. They can greet people with smiles and warmth that the physician may not do. They can assure patients that things will be okay, and they can explain procedures. Of course, the nurses do more than this. They are highly skilled healthcare professionals who have vast healthcare knowledge that they put to use each day. When it comes to many of the day-to-day operations on a unit or in a clinic, the nurses are the ones who do the bulk of the work and who know how to perform all of the necessary clinical procedures with precision.

Nursing Options in Various Fields

Nursing is an in demand job, and that's another reasons why it is such a great profession to choose today. Pay is great at all levels of nursing, and as mentioned earlier, you will discover that you have a host of different choices if you find that you want to specialize in a field of nursing.

Those who want to work with children should look into specializing as a pediatric nurse. If you would rather work with the elderly, becoming a geriatric nurse is possible. Surgical nurses will work alongside surgeons, and nurse anesthetists will help to administer anesthesia to patients. Because surgical and intensive care nursing require specialized knowledge, they often pay more. A nurse might choose to specialize in oncology, medical/surgical, OB/GYN, or any number of different nursing specialty areas. The possibilities are nearly limitless.

Those who receive their nursing degree will find some other opportunities, as well. They may want to work as a home care provider, working with just one patient, or a handful of patients in their own homes. Working as a travel nurse is another possibility. Most of the time, the travel nurses will go to various parts of the country for several month stints where they work in a hospital, clinic, or other area that needs them. This type of nursing job can be a fun and interesting option for those who are up for a bit of adventure in their lives.

Start Making a Difference

The road to becoming a nurse is a long one, and it is going to require quite a bit of education. However, the proper education will prepare you for the demanding career of nursing. You have a plethora of different career paths available to you when you start your nursing degree, and you are going to be able to work in a career that is interesting, challenging, and that will provide you with great remuneration.

You want to become a nurse so you can make a difference. There is nothing stopping you. Learn more about what you need to start doing right now in order to become a nurse and start your career. Take the leap and jump onto the right career path.

Nurses change the lives of everyone around them. They are going to make their lives better and easier for their patients, as well as the families of those patients. This is quite helpful when a family has fears and does not know what is happening with their loved one. The calm and comforting presence of a nurse can make quite a difference. They are also going to be able to assist the physician. Becoming a nurse is a noble choice, but it does take a special type of person to excel in this profession. Hard work is par for the course when it comes to nursing.

Compensation for nurses working full time according to the Bureau of Labor often are in the mid $70,000 and higher depending on experience, education, and specialty. There are over 104 different specialties with a number of them requiring higher degrees. Given these opportunities along with appropriate education and experience nurses can move laterally and horizontally into other specialties and positions.

The long hours, particularly for hospital based nurses, stress associated with dealing with often life and death situations that accompany the profession can lead to burn out. It is critical as you begin your profession learning how to balance these demands to ensure adequate time for yourself, family and friends.

Bottom line, if are you a caring person interested in helping others, committed to a lifetime of service to assist others nursing is one of the most emotionally awarding careers in health care.   The *Johnson and Johnson Campaign for Nursing Future* is a great resource to learn more about nursing. Click on this link Discover Nursing.

CHAPTER TWO

Getting Ready for Nursing School

High School Preparation

High school preparation that includes completing science and math courses provide the foundation for success in the nursing curriculum. Taking these courses is critical. These core courses provide the foundation for success in the nursing program. Some high schools have health academies that are designed specifically for students interested in seeking health careers. These are good options for students who know the career they want to pursue. A number of health academies offer practical or in some states they are referred to as vocational nurse programs. The high school practical nurse programs are a great option for students who want to become a registered nurse or for some who desire to remain as a practical nurse. The practical nurse educational courses and clinical experiences provide a strong foundation for those students who want to seek an educational program leading to eligibility for registered nurse licensure.

Which School of Nursing and Degree Path Should I Apply Too

Deciding which school to apply to is also a major task. In part the decision lies on the type of nursing degree you want to obtain. (See below on degree options). Many community colleges, universities, some hospitals, and private not-for-profit and for-profit colleges and universities offer nursing programs. There are pros and cons of each option. Typically public-sector community colleges and universities have waiting lists for students who want to enter into the nursing program. This means that students typically must complete all of the prerequisites required for entry, apply, and if not competitive go onto a waiting list. Depending on the demand for enrollments a student with, for example, a grade point average (GPA) of 3.0 could theoretically wait 2 to 3 years in order to be admitted to a two-year associate degree or a pre-licensure bachelor of science in nursing (BSN) program.

Private universities on the other hand typically do not have extensive waiting list. The disadvantage, if any, is the costs associated with the programs. Given that private colleges and universities do not receive public funds the student tuition and fees must support the operation of the school. These schools present a viable alternative and typically most have financing options which will allow the student to attend school full-time. While there has been some negative publicity about some of these for-profit schools the vast majority provide a high quality education. The publicity is largely unjustified and given the substantial wait that most students have to endure to achieve a nursing degree from a public university, they are a viable alternative.

Choosing your initial degree path be it practical nurse, diploma, associate degree, or bachelor of science nurse (BSN) is the first step. The route you choose will depend on availability of financial support, the time commitment that you want to make to your education, and your career goals. For some students the practical nurse program, which is typically 12 months in length, is the best place to start. Becoming licensed allows you to begin as a practical or vocational nurse and then seek admission later to an associate degree program as a registered nurse. After graduating from an associate degree program, you'll be eligible to take the NCLEX RN® examination. Passing this exam allows you to apply to the State Board of Nursing for a license as a registered nurse (RN). For licensed practical nurses or licensed vocational nurses (LPN or LVN) the exam is NCLEX PN®. As with the RN exam achieving the passing score allows you to apply for a license as a practical nurse.

Starting as a practical nurse provides a career ladder option for students who have limited time to go to school and/or financials support to afford such. There are number of programs which allow a practical nurse to enter into the associate degree program. Once you have completed your associate degree and find that you're ready to continue on for your bachelor of science degree then you can enroll in a RN to BSN program. These programs are designed to award credit for your associate degree. A student takes additional upper division general education courses required to obtain a bachelor of science in nursing degree. The upper division nursing courses include, among others, community health, research and evidence-based practice as well as management and leadership.

Another option seen less common is a hospital based diploma program for registered nurses. These programs typically take up to three years to complete. Many are also associated with a community college for the general education and science courses. There are usually additional clinical hours required in the diploma programs than found in associate degree and bachelor of science in nursing programs. These graduates typically work in hospital nursing. The diploma graduates are eligible to take the RN license exam.

Some students may decide to enter directly into the associate degree program. These programs are typically two years in length. This is a faster track to achieve a RN license. However, if your goal is to eventually get into management or achieve a graduate degree and for example want to become a nurse practitioner, you will need to obtain your BSN degree. A number of hospitals who are seeking magnet status (special recognition for excellence in nursing care) may require their nurses to have a BSN or achieve one within so many years after being hired. In some cases these hospitals may choose to hire BSN nurses over associate degree.

The good news is, associate degree nurses can easily obtain their BSN degree through a variety of RN to BSN programs that are readily available. Some are online and others are delivered in a hybrid model which allows you to attend classes both on campus and online. The latter model allows you to have interaction with expert faculty on campus as well as to access all of the campus based resources. Online on the other hand relies on the students' motivation to work fairly independently in completing the course requirements. This program however, is definitely not self paced.

Another option is to enter directly into a pre–licensure BSN program. These are typically four years in length. Unlike the associate degree programs which allow you to set for the registered nurse exam at the end of your first two years of education and then work and go to school, the pre-licensure BSN does not afford that option. However, depending on your life situation including your financial resources the pre-licensure BSN program is a preferred choice for many individuals.

Another pre-licensure BSN option is a "fast track/accelerated" option. In this program a student who has an associate of sciences/arts degree or a bachelor of science/art and has completed the required science courses for nursing can enter directly into the BSN degree track. These programs are typically accelerated and will allow the student to complete his BSN within 12 to 18 months. The course work is fast paced and requires the student's full attention in order to be successful. This program is an excellent option for second degree students who want to achieve a BSN in a short period of time.

The last option, seen somewhat infrequently, is a master entry-level program. In these pre-licensure programs in which the students typically already has a baccalaureate degree in a non nursing area and exits the program with the master of science in nursing and takes the RN licensing exam upon graduation.

Regulatory and Accreditation For Your Nursing School

Nursing schools are a part of a college or university. In some cases with practical nurse programs they may be a part of a technical school. No matter what the name of the parent unit in which the school is located all must be approved by a state agency that regulates higher education. The college, university, trade school if they are going to participate in Title IV funding provided by US Department of Education must also be approved by this agency. The Title IV allows the college, university or technical school to participate in the Pell grant program (more about Pell grants later), as well as other Federal affiliated loan guarantees.

Regional Accrediting Organizations and National Accrediting Organization

Most public schools are regionally accredited by one of the six main accrediting agencies depending on the physical location of the main campus. Technical colleges, trade schools and other for-profit schools are usually accredited by one of the national accrediting organizations. All accrediting agencies must be approved by the US Department of Education. Regional accredited colleges and universities often will not accept transfer credits from colleges, trade and career schools that are accredited by national accrediting organizations. This restriction is not imposed by the US Department of Education. Frequently restrictions on the acceptance of credits stems from a lack of understanding of the national accrediting approval process required by the US Department of Education who authorizes these agencies. Regionally accredited organizations cite a reason for not accepting transfer credits is because national accrediting agencies lack adequate standards to insure qualified faculty and library resources in their accredited schools.   In reality, both are accredited by the US Department of Education using the same standards.   Logically the Federal government would not allow taxpayer funds to be awarded to any schools unable to meet their standards.   More information can be found at the following links:

Accrediting Agencies in the United States and at Information about Regional Accreditation

State Board of Nursing and Licensing Examination

All nursing programs that prepare graduates for the practical or registered nurses licensing examination must be approved by the state board of nursing. As mentioned previously this licensing exam is called the NCLEX®RN for registered nurses or NCLEX® PN for practical nurses. NCLEX® is the acronym for the National Council Licensure Examination. This examination is developed and owned by the National Council of State Boards of Nursing, Inc. This Council is comprised of all 50 states and four of the US territories. They administer the NCLEX® on behalf of their member states and territories.

The NCLEX® assesses an individual's knowledge, abilities, and skills necessary to be an effective and safe practitioner at the entry-level.   The exam uses a computerized adaptive testing (CAT) format that is administered by Pearson VUE in their Pearson professional centers.

Test Plan – NCLEX® PN

The exam's content is based on patient needs:

Safe Effective Care Environment

Management of Care

Safety and Infection Control

Health Promotion and Maintenance

Psychosocial integrity
Physiology integrity
Basic Care and Comfort
Pharmacological and Parenteral Therapies
Reduction of Risk Potential
Physiological

More specific details can be found at the National Council of State Board of Nursing website:

PN Detailed Test Plan

Test Plan – NCLEX® RN
Safe Effective Care Environment
Coordinator of Care
Safety and Infection Control
Health Promotion and Maintenance
Psychosocial integrity
Physiological integrity
Basic Care and Comfort
Phamacological Therapies
Reduction in Risk Potential
Physiological Adaptation
Psychiatric

More specific details can be found at the National Council of State Board of Nursing website:
RN Detailed Test Plan

In some states there are separate boards for practical nurses and registered nurses. The board of nursing has prescribed standards that nursing schools must follow in order to be approved. Therefore, it is critical that your school has and maintains the state board of nursing approval. It is against state laws for any program to identify themselves as a nursing school if they are not approved by the appropriate board of nursing. The boards of nursing does approve schools that have both regional and national accreditation.

Boards of nursing do have the authority to periodically review all nursing programs. The regulations regarding such reviews vary state-by-state. When considering a school, it is important to check its approval status on the board of nursing website.

The nursing program may have only initial approval until they have achieved success in having their graduate pass the NCLEX® exam. Those schools which consistently have low passing scores on the licensing exam may lose their state approval. Therefore, it's important that you check the regulatory status of the school to which you are applying.

On the board of nursing website you can also find the licensing pass rates for your particular school. The board lists in alphabetical order by program type all of the approved schools in the state. A quick review will reveal how successful your school has been in preparing students to successfully pass the licensing exam.

Nursing Program Accreditation

There are two major program accreditation agencies that are specific to nursing schools. They are the National League for Nursing Accreditation Commission (NLNAC) and the Commission on Collegiate Nursing Education (CCNE). NLNAC accredits practical nurse, associate degree, baccalaureate, master and doctoral programs. CCNE only accredits baccalaureate, master's and doctoral programs. These are voluntary agencies and provide an external review of a schools compliance with a predefined set of standards. The program accreditation standards in some cases, mirror those of State boards of nursing and/or are similar. In some states, the boards of nursing require program accreditation for schools to maintain approval. These program accrediting agencies must also be approved by the US Department of Education. For some schools they serve as the accreditor for Title IV funding.

Program accreditation is not required. Many new schools have to complete an application and a lengthy review process prior to being eligible for accreditation. It is not uncommon to find new schools unaccredited. However, many will have candidacy status while seeking full approval. It is an additional gold seal of approval. The most critical consideration is that your program is approved by your respective state board of nursing. Many practical nurse and associate degree programs do not seek this voluntary accreditation, primarily due to the costs associated with such and the expenses that must be incurred to achieve and maintain approval.

Admission Requirements

A diploma from a recognized state approved high school or general education degree (GED) is required for admission to all nursing schools. Most also require an assessment of English grammar and reading comprehension as well as math skills. Depending on the program type the level of the competency expectation may vary. The two most common assessments used for nursing students are the Test of Essential Academic Skills (TEAS) and the Health Information Systems, Inc. (HESI) A2. Information on these assessments may be found at ATI Testing for TEAS and HEIS A2 Testing for the A2. The cutoff score for admission depends on the program type and demand for students.

For most public sector programs the high school grade point average is of utmost importance for those programs that admit students directly from high school. For those schools that require students to complete the prerequisites prior to admission, the college grade-point average, particularly the science courses is usually a critical variable.

Some programs require a written essay from the applicant. They may ask why you are interested in attending nursing school or similar questions. In addition they may also require a personal interview. Given the subjective nature of these assessments it is reasonable for you to inquire with the admissions representative how the essays and interviews are scored. It would be useful to ask for a copy of their scoring rubrics. They may or may not provide evaluation criteria; however, it would be useful to understand how the school's admissions committee uses this information to evaluate your application.

Most public sector programs have more applicants than spaces for new students. As a result they will use a variety of factors to rank applicants. The students are then admitted in the order of their ranking protocol. While private for-profit schools, typically admit three or four times a year generally do not have waiting lists. The drawback, of course, is the cost between the two programs. However, if your goal is to achieve your nursing license in a relatively short period of time, the investment will most likely pay for itself in a short period of time.

Tuition and Fees
Almost all nursing programs, in addition to the standard tuition have a variety of fees. The fees depending on the college or university may include books, uniforms, supply kits, health insurance, immunizations, criminal background checks and so forth. All schools and in particular private schools are required to provide a detailed list of tuition and fees. There will be a variation among tuition and fees depending on the geographical location of your school, demand for the program, program type, and if it is a public sector or a for-profit school.

Financial Aid
To ensure you have adequate finances while in school, it is essential to meet with the financial aid advisor. The advisor will review your situation to determine what financial aid options for which you are eligible. Depending on your situation, you may be eligible for Pell grants

(money from the Federal government that does not have to be paid back), a variety of federally guaranteed loans, private loans, scholarships, and work-study opportunities while in school. There may be tuition assistance if you qualify for any special programs. In most cases you do not have to start paying back the loans until after you have graduate. These loans are typically at a very low interest rate and make the cost of education affordable as they are spread out in some cases up to 10 years or more.

It's critical that the funding of your school is planned so you will be able to spend your time focusing on your education. You'll be required to fill out the Free Application for Federal Student Aid (FAFSA). This form is used to determine your eligibility for student financial aid including Pell grants, federal work study, and federal student loans. The application is used as the primary form for the various federal student aid programs, state-based aid as well as institutional assistance when available.

FAFSA has several different student aid options. The most common are:

Pell grants - current funding level provides up to $5,550 per year in aid for students with low expected family contribution. The amount of funding varies each year depending on the appropriations from Congress.

Stafford loans - a loan which may have subsidize or unsubsidized interest payments. If subsidized the federal government pays for the interest while the student is enrolled at least 50% time in an educational program. If unsubsidized the interests accumulates on the loan.

Perkins loan - is similar to the Stafford loan that is given directly by the school if Title IV eligible.

Federal Work Study Program - allow students to work part-time up to a certain amount of hours and the federal government pays up to 75% of their wages.

More information on Federal student aid can be found at this website: Free Application for Federal Student Aid

Loan Repayment Options

The Nursing Educational Loan Repayment Program is designed to repay student loans if the nurse works in a Critical Shortage Facility. If the nurses works a minimum of two years in an eligible Critical Shortage Facility in the designated mental health or primary care Health Professional Shortage Area (HPSA), the Federal government will pay up to 60% of qualifying loans balance. There is a possibility of extending the payment one more year for another 25% repayment. More information can be found at HRSA Loans and Scholarships.

In November 2012, the US Department of Education announced a new loan repayment program. This plan is known as *"Pay As You Earn"* that links the loan repayments to 10% of the borrowers' discretionary income with any remaining balance forgiven after 20 years. This new program only applies to individuals who took loans out in or after the fiscal year which is between the dates of October 1, 2011 to September 30, 2012.

Those that do not qualify can still apply for the older loan program that is pegged at 15% of discretionary income and forgiveness after 25 years. These are alternative to the regular 10 year repayment plan. More information can be found at US Department of Education Student Loans.

Various states also have loan forgiveness programs with varying payment back terms. Most of the military services, Indian Health Services as well as Veteran Affairs also have loan payback programs. A Goggle search is the best method to learn about current programs and eligibility requirements in regards to these options.

Bottom line, with planning and flexibility to move to a Critical Shortage Area, there are a number of loan repayments options for nursing students. These options should make private schools more attractive given the potential support for loan forgiveness, thus by-passing long waiting lists found at many public sector schools.

CHAPTER THREE

After Being Admitted

Attend orientation to learn exactly the expectations of a student, understand the curriculum and other requirements. The orientation is typically given prior to the start of the term. It's absolutely essential that you attend the orientation. In some schools they have a separate orientation that includes the family and significant others. If your school doesn't have such it is recommended that you ask for an orientation specifically geared to those who will be supporting you in the program. It's critical that your support systems understand the curriculum, the financing and costs associated with going to school and how your life as a nursing student is going to change. Nursing school is a very demanding and time-consuming major. School may mean at times giving up special events associated with family celebrations and the like because you have a test the next day. You may also find that free time to watch television, going out to dinner with friends, shopping, maybe limited. Thus, getting the family and/or significant others to understand the importance of your schooling and how you all need to work together is critical to your success.

In the orientation you'll receive an overview of the expectations of a student as well as participate in a discussion regarding the catalog and student handbook. These will be the rules and regulations that you will need to abide by as you progress in your degree plan. Most programs will require you to sign an acknowledgment of receipt of the catalog and student handbook. Thus it's extremely important that you read these documents. If you have any questions ask them prior to beginning your nursing program. These documents serve as the legal contract between you and the school in regards to your education.

In some private for-profit schools they will require you to sign an enrollment agreement. The agreement typically specifies your tuition and fees, the refund policies and procedures, and arbitration clauses if there are any disputes related to your education. Unlike public sector schools, private schools typically are required by law to have much more disclosure about the tuition and fees, refund policies, student expectations, and time it takes a typical student to complete the plan of study. They also are required to provide student placement rates after they've graduated from the program, passing rates on licensing examinations and so forth.

The catalog typically contains information about the college including its administrative team, state approvals and accreditations. They also have information regarding admission requirements for the various degrees, tuition and fees associated with the various majors, transfer credit policy, graduation requirements and information about the various degree programs.

The catalog also describes the curriculum in detail. This is where you'll find information about the degree plan, course numbers, credits and course descriptions. Most schools have both a full-time and a part-time degree plan identified for nursing. There is information about the grading scale and progression requirements in order to successfully complete the program of study. There is also an academic calendar. Admission requirements for nurses include clinical health requirements (immunizations and CPR card) and criminal background checks. These requirements will be found in the catalog and/or in the student handbook. In almost all cases these requirements usually have to be completed prior to being officially admitted to the nursing program.

Many nursing programs do not allow rounding up of grades. Most schools have a specific cutoff score that the student needs to achieve in order to be successful. The rules are usually rigidly enforced, as the student either achieves the score or he/she doesn't. There's information about how to withdraw from those course, how to request a leave of absence, and how the final grades are computed and posted. Many nursing programs will have a two course failure policy. This means if you have failed two of any required courses, you are automatically dismissed from the program.

Most nursing programs also have a comprehensive examination either at the end of the degree plan or within the last course. This exam is a predictor of your success on passing on the first attempt the NCLEX®. Generally these are a pass/fail requirement. If you fail the comprehensive examination you would be required to repeat the final capstone course. The protocols around administering the capstone examination vary with different schools. Most will provide you at least one or two opportunities to achieve an acceptable score. The required score is usually identified in the capstone course syllabus. In some cases it may be listed in the catalog.

The student handbook is a guide for nursing students once they are enrolled in the program. Typically the handbook contains the philosophy of the nursing program and the student learning outcomes that drive the curriculum. It may also include information regarding the nursing curriculum similar to what was found in the catalog. There will be information about student participation in program governance. In most programs, students participate in the curriculum committee as well as student advisory groups. There will also be a section on health requirements as well as the policy related to students with a disability.

Most handbooks will also have a section on academic standards and policy. This includes such items as academic integrity, attendance requirements, and examination policies, the use of external testing, and management of repeating a missed exam as well as how late assignments are handled. It also may address the grading policy and incomplete grades. Information about the student dress code and conduct is also typically found in the handbook. The appendix will also have specific policies that are designed to guide the student, primarily in the clinical setting.

Health insurance may be required as well as student malpractice insurance. The student malpractice insurance is usually a small fee that covers you for any acts of negligence or malpractice in your role as a student. You are to never to function independently without faculty supervision so the odds of any untoward event occurring are limited.

Criminal background checks are required by the school of nursing for two primary reasons. The first is the clinical agencies where you will do your practice require the school does not send any student or faculty member to their site unless he/she has a cleared background. This is required to protect the public given that nurses will have access to personal information of patients who may be vulnerable. All state boards of nursing require a cleared criminal background check prior to granting the applicant to apply for a nursing license. The background check typically includes the following:

- Social security number verification
- Criminal search (7 years or up to 5 county criminal searches)
- Employment verification (for students with a previous professional health care license)
- Violent Sexual Offender and Predator Registry Search

- Office of Inspector General List of excluded Individuals/Entities
- General Services Administration List of Parties Excluded from Federal Programs
- US Treasury, Office of Foreign Assets Control (OFAC), List of Specially Designated Nations (SDN)

Deferred adjudications and pending cases are included in the criminal search section of the report. Any falsification of information will result in immediate removal of you from the school of nursing.

If there are any criminal charges pending and/or you have been convicted of such proof of having completed any conditions of sentencing and/or probation must be provided. Typically students who have successful completed the terms of the deferred adjudication agreement may not be disqualified. *It is very important if any of these situations apply to you that you address your concerns with the admission representative.* Some states such as Texas provide the criminal background check of nursing school applicants. Those who are found to have a disqualifying charge can then work with the board of nursing to seek a resolution prior to be admitting to the nursing program.

If the check reveals a disqualifying event it is your burden to produce substantial evidence that proves the crimes charged are incorrect. Most programs allow the student up to one year to resolve the issue. There are no guarantees that if the school should clear you for enrollment that a clinical agency or the state board of nursing will accept you as a student or as a candidate for registration, permit, or license.

If any changes should occur in your criminal background status while in school, typically you are required to notify them as soon as possible. The most frequent violations that occur are driving while intoxicated or for possession of an illicit drug such as marijuana. As shared depending on the state and clinical agency agreements even if you are convicted it may mean you're not able to attend clinical rotations and/or be permitted to apply for a license as a nurse. The same rule may also apply if charges are pending. The importance of having even a minor infraction cannot be underestimated. Without being able to attend clinical rotations, you will be unable to complete successfully the nursing program. Therefore, when tempted with excessive alcohol, marijuana use or take prescription medications which are not prescribed to you, keep in mind the consequences of those actions may have on your education and eventual goal to become a nurse.

CHAPTER FOUR

What You're Going to Need When You Start Nursing School

Textbooks

Textbooks are going to be expensive and will be critically important for your learning throughout the curriculum. Particularly in the for-profit schools the textbooks are included in the student's financial aid package. This option may also be available in the public sector schools as well. Do not attempt to get by without purchasing textbooks as you simply will not be successful in the curriculum. *Ebooks* are common and most have the ability to be downloaded to a laptop or mobile device. There are many advantages to the e-books as they have hyperlinks, video clips, and ability to tag information, and underline important concepts. An example of a eBook can be found on Elsevier webpage: Elsevier They are one of the world's largest publishers of nursing textbooks.

Computer, Printer and Smartphone

A laptop is preferable given it allows you mobility. You can take the laptop to class for typing notes as well as have ready access to your *Ebooks* and other online resources. Having a wireless Internet connection is also critical as this allows you to access Internet resources where ever you may be. All of the major mobile phone carriers have wireless internet options. Having a computer with adequate battery life is also important because many times classrooms do not have sufficient electrical outlets to charge your batteries.

A number of nursing programs may include a laptop as a part of your fees. This option is particularly available to students enrolling in programs that have a significant online component. The laptops typically come complete with Microsoft Office Suite®, Internet Explorer®, and other programs necessary for your use in the program. Many schools that provide the laptops have made available 24/7 support for any issues related to the using the computers as well as 48 hours replacement policies if the computer should malfunction. Schools cannot require you to purchase their specific laptops. However, given they come fully loaded with the software needed and support services, the option is a good value for many students.

Invest in a good inkjet printer as one is needed to print papers, Internet web searches, email, and email attachments, etc. A wireless printer has many advantages given you can print documents from your lab top when you are not connected via a cable. A high speed printer is worth the slightly increased cost.

You should have access to a smart phone as well. You will be able to download drug information, common laboratory tests, medical dictionary, drug guides including drug calculations and access many of your textbooks. This allows you to access this information while in your clinical environment. You will have at your fingertips access to the most current information to aid you in providing nursing care. Some nursing schools have created special smart phone packages that can be purchase directly from a vendor such as *Skyscape*. Their link is Skyscape Their applications are very useful.

Be aware it is absolutely forbidden for you to use the camera on your smart phone to take pictures of patients, families and visitors, or patient records. Taking pictures is considered a breach of patient confidentiality and can lead to your dismissal from the nursing program if these violations occur. In addition, you could also be subject to civil lawsuits because of invasion of patient privacy. Nursing schools as well as the clinical agencies typically require students to sign confidentiality agreements prior to attending the clinical rotation.

Social media policies are also common. These policies cover the use of such internet applications as Facebook, Twetter, Linkedin, and You Tube. The American Nurses Association (ANA) e-publication, *Principles for Social Networking and the Nurse: Guidance for the Registered Nurse* was released in September 2012. The e-publication incorporates the *ANA Code of Ethics, Social Policy Statement, and Nursing: Scope and Standards of Practice*. When social media is used inappropriate nurses as well as students can face legal issues, potential adverse actions with boards of nursing, and even fired by their employer and for students dismissed from nursing school. The ANA book can be found at: Principles for Social Networking and Nurse: Guidance for the Registered Nurse

Uniforms and Shoes

You are going to need at least three sets of uniforms. Some schools prescribe the uniforms that you are to wear and many include the initial set of uniforms in your fees. All will have a nursing school patch that will need to be sewn onto the sleeve of the uniform. You'll also need a name tag. In your orientation this information will be shared with you. Having well fitting shoes that are comfortable is critical. As a nursing student while at the clinical site you'll be on your feet almost continuously. So to ensure more comfort do not skimp on the purchase of good shoes. Again, during your new student orientation, the school will give you the parameters concerning types of shoes you should wear.

Also be aware that most programs have personal appearance (including tattoos) and dress codes. Usually there can be no dangling earrings, no visible piercings, and requirements how you are to wear your hair. All of these requirements are designed to begin instilling in the student the professional appearance and behavior expected of a nurse. Being a nurse is serious business and one must dress and act in a professional manner. The public expects nurses to adhere to a high standard. The role modeling begins while in nursing school. Thus, there will be an emphasis throughout nursing school on professional appearance and behaviors. Students are often evaluated throughout their nursing program on professional appearance and behaviors.

Nursing Supply Kit

You will be required to purchase a supply kit when you start the program. The kit includes such things as a stethoscope, syringes, catheters, gloves, blood pressure cuff, and other types of medical supplies you will need to use in your clinical skills labs. The school will also have some supplies available to the skills labs. However, the students are typically expected to have the supplies that they're going to need to practice the various required skills. The bookstore usually sells the kits or they can be ordered from a vendor such as *Pocket Nurse*. Their link is Pocket Nurse

CHAPTER FIVE

Understanding the Curriculum

Most nursing curriculums are similar. Practical nurse curriculums are typically 12 months in length and include a variety of courses designed to prepare the graduate to be successful on the licensing examination. Courses will include anatomy and physiology, fundamentals of nutrition, human growth and development, foundations of nursing, medical surgical nursing and a variety of specialty courses. The specialty courses include maternal child health and psychiatric nursing. Some of the cutting edge practical nurse programs will also include gerontology, informatics, community health, and leadership.

The RN diploma, ADN and BSN programs have similar nursing content. However, the student learning outcomes for RN programs are at a higher level as reflected in the scope of practice of registered nurses. The BSN programs have additional coursework in community health, research or evidence-based practice, and leadership and management. General education courses including humanities, social sciences, math, and other science courses are also required in the ADN and BSN in nursing programs. As with any college degree a number of credits includes college core courses as well as in those in the major.

It's important to closely review the college catalog to determine the number of required credits for the degree which you are seeking. Credits vary widely in the number required. The curriculums with a higher number of credits means it takes longer to complete the requirements and are more costly. Many public sector schools have been mandated by their legislatures to decrease the number of credits. This has forced the curriculums to be more focused so students obtain the essential content. This action has stopped credit creep which has contributed to the higher cost of education and of course the time it takes to complete the degree.

Typical Sequence of Courses

Generally the coursework starts with the science and liberal art courses. Most difficult of these courses is anatomy and physiology, nutrition, biology, and math. Some BSN students also struggle with chemistry. With the exception of practical nurse programs, there are generally two anatomy and physiology courses required. Many programs require that you have to achieve at least a C+ or higher in the science courses in order to progress in the nursing curriculum. Thus it is critically important that you do well in these courses.

Once the science pre-requisites are out of the way, students then start taking the nursing courses. Some programs require the student to complete the science and liberal art pre-requisites courses prior to applying to the nursing program. The first nursing courses, depending on the curriculum, are generally pharmacology, health assessment and foundations of nursing. These are critical courses as they provide the foundation needed to progress in the curriculum. Learning how to do an appropriate health assessment is critical. Pharmacology that includes calculating dosages of medications is probably one of the more important courses in the curriculum. As nurses, much of your practice activities are related to pharmacology. The foundation courses provide the necessary clinical skills applicable to progress in the curriculum. The foundation courses will include substantial hours in the skills lab and simulation center learning how to safely perform a variety of procedures. Health assessment is usually something students enjoy as it is practically focused and useful. Foundation takes a lot of time because new medical terms are introduced as well as how to safely perform a variety of skills critical to the practice of nursing.

The next two challenging courses are medical/surgical nursing. These courses are the heart of nursing practice. Close to 85% of NCLEX® questions come from content taught in these courses. Frequently maternal nursing or pediatrics will be taught the same term as the first medical/surgical course. The following term typically has a second medical/surgical course along with a course such as the community nursing concepts followed by leadership and management and perhaps mental health nursing. Almost all curriculums have a capstone course in the last term of the program. The capstone course typically has a practice focus. The student may attend some classroom didactic sessions primarily related to reviewing of medical/surgical concepts as well as material to assist the student in preparing for the NCLEX® exam.

With the exception of leadership and management courses most curriculums in nursing include a clinical practicum. The practicum varies in hours depending on the number of course credits. Significant hours are devoted to medical/surgical nursing practice given this again is the bulk of nursing practice. Included in the clinical practice hours are also simulation experiences. The majority of schools in the country have simulation mannequins with associated software applications designed to assist the student in gaining competence and managing a variety of medical/surgical, maternity, and pediatric clinical situations. Typically these clinical experiences (at least for registered nurses) occur primarily in acute care settings. Practical nurses may receive much of their training in long-term care facilities, home health and/or in subacute units (This level of care is for patients who do not need a hospital level of acute care but do need a higher level of care that can be provided in skilled nursing facility).

It's a challenge for practical nurses to find practice sites within acute care settings given that most of these agencies do not allow the students in their facilities. This is primarily because practical nurses are not employed by acute care hospitals as their practice sites are typically long term care, home health, and subacute settings.

Bottom line, it's critical to do well in the science prerequisite courses. In some programs as mentioned previously, the grade point average (GPA) in these courses is the gatekeeper for admission to the program. In other programs these courses are taken after you are admitted. The second major hurdle is ensuring you have an adequate foundation in pharmacology, foundations of nursing, and medical/surgical nursing. The bulk of your practice as a nurse will come from the information that you learned in these courses.

CHAPTER SIX

How to Successfully Master the Content

All nursing curriculums are guided by a student learning outcomes. These outcomes can be found in the catalog as well as in the student handbook. They are the guidelines for the content that is delivered throughout the curriculum. It is critical you become familiar with these outcomes and understand what is being asked for in such. Each course in the curriculum has a description followed by the objectives. The course description and objectives are directly linked to the student learning outcomes defined for the entire nursing curriculum. Weekly assignments indicated in your syllabus as well as the topical outline should be directly linked to a specific course objectives or objectives. Most syllabi will indicate the weekly topic and directly linked this information back to the course objectives. In many cases they also link the course objective back to the student learning objectives for the entire curriculum. Review the course objectives and topical outline to aid in understanding which topics are of higher priority.

Many programs also include weekly homework assignments in which students have to complete NCLEX® style questions related to the topic. This is a sound evidence-based approach to improving your comprehension and understanding of the concepts you are studying. The research recommends students complete a minimum of 2,000-2,500 questions for average students and 3,000-4,000 for at-risk students (McDowell, 2007; Firth, Sewell, & Clark, 2005; McQueen, Shelton, &

Zimmerman, 2004; Stark, Feikema, Wyngarten, 2002; Williams & Bryant, 2001). You should strive to complete at least 50 questions per week and aim for getting 90% correct. You can use several different NCLEX® books to provide variety of questions. The books typically have CDs or online resources that you can access to complete the assessments.

Various schools use external vendors such as Assessment Technology Institute (ATI), Health Information Systems, Inc. (HESI), and Kaplan Nursing to support student learning. All have support material specific for different nursing courses. If your program doesn't use one of these vendors, you should strongly recommend through your Nursing Student Advisory Council they recommend these learning resources be made available. While the vendors have different approaches to supporting student learning the basic information is the same. Many of the supporting material include case studies and adaptive testing, as well as supplemental readings to support student learning. Case studies are particularly helpful as they develop comprehensive critical thinking skills.

The teacher made examinations should follow the course objectives which should be linked to the test plan. Initially test questions will have more emphasis on knowledge. The content becomes more complex and as you progress in the curriculum, the questions will advance to application and critical thinking. The questions progressively become more and more complex as you move through the curriculum. As previously shared, critical courses are pharmacology, foundations and medical/surgical courses. Up to 85% of the questions on NCLEX examination come from this content. This focus is a priority because the majority of patients who you will care for as a nurse will be those with medical/surgical conditions. Thus the entry level nurse must be competent to provide care to these patients. Specialty focus on community health, leadership, pediatrics, maternity and psychiatric/mental health conditions is secondary.

Many nursing curriculum use what is known as concept mapping. This is an integration of nursing and physiological concepts into the curriculum. The information may be a bit confusing as the language is often not coached in medical terms. The idea is for the student to be competent in understanding the key concepts needed to provide safe and competent patient care. Therefore, it's essential that in your readings in preparing for a class that you are following the course objectives and linking it back to the concepts being discussed.

Test Taking Strategies

Faculty writes examinations to test your knowledge of the content being taught. As previously shared, the faculty created exams should be linked to the student learning outcomes which are in term directly related to course objectives. The questions for the most part should follow the NCLEX® format that uses a multiple-choice format and some of the alternate format questions. Alternative format questions may include an audio file in which the student needs to correctly identify the sounds. Typical sounds are of the heart and lungs. The faculty developed test items similar to the NCLEX® format should contain higher levels of cognition that progress from remembering, memorization, understanding, applying, analyzing, and evaluating. The faculty should introduce NCLEX style questions early in the curriculum in such courses as health assessment and fundamentals. As shared the questions will increase in complexity as you progress in the curriculum.

Remembering - facts and figures are things that you must remember in order to have the foundation for your nursing practice. This content is typically found in your foundations course. Knowledge is critical as it is the foundation from which you make critical decisions.

Understanding - memorizing information needs to be accompanied by an understanding of the factual knowledge. A translation of that knowledge into a patient's situation is an important step in being able to apply such to the care of patients.

Applying - this step requires a higher level of understanding of the information in that you must use your knowledge and understanding in patient care situations.

Analyzing - you must know, understand and be able to apply the information. Analyzing is critical as you make decisions about patient care. Without the ability to analyze knowledge, understand it and apply it in patient care and you will be unable to be successful.

Evaluating - using the four steps described you then need to be able to evaluate your decisions based on your assessments and interventions.

Example of Cognition Application
Remembering – remember the classification of the drug Paxil (paroxetine hyrochloride)

Understanding – develop an understanding of action of Paxil (paroxetine hyrochloride)

Applying – identify specific situations how Paxil (paroxetine hyrochloride) would be used to care for the patient

Analyzing – knowing the difference in side effects of Paxil (paroxetine hyrochloride) and other medications.

Evaluating – what is the expected outcomes of Paxil (paroxetine hyrochloride)

As with any examination, the key strategy for success is preparation. It's critical that you take time to prepare for the examination that is scheduled. A quiet place free from interruption that allows you to concentrate on the material is ideal. Take advantage of the school's library or other public libraries as a place to study. Studying at home can be challenging given interruptions that inadvertently occur. Preparing for an exam should have the same priority as going to work and performing your duties as your employer would expect. Cramming the night before the examination is a sure route to failure. In nursing school there are significant numbers of pages to be read prior to each class. It is essential that you keep up with the reading so when it comes time for preparing for the exam, you are reviewing your highlights and notes.

Get a good nights' sleep before the examination and avoid use of high levels of caffeine or mind alternating medications. Feeling tired and drowsy during the examination is clearly not what you want. Associate with students who tend to be positive and self assured.

The key to studying is to learn how to concentrate on the material that is important and not spending time on content less critical. The course objectives and weekly assignments provide some guidance regarding which material is more important than others. Some faculty provides study guides which may be useful. In those programs that use nursing learning material created by outside companies such as Kaplan, ATI, and HESI this information may be helpful. These educational companies typically have supplemental learning material that includes case studies, review questions, NCLEX® preparation resources and additional reading material. Their learning resources may be more concise and focused than that found in your nursing textbooks.

Reading the assignments prior to lecture will aid in your understanding of the material. Take notes in class and actively engaged in questions so you can have an opportunity to understand the content. It's also important to read your notes after class. This will save you time later on when you are studying for the examinations. Take advantage of tutoring services if made available. There are a couple of external tutoring services that you may find helpful such as **Net Tutor** Their link is Nettutor . **Smart Thinking** link is Smart Thinking. Typically these services are contracted by your school of nursing. If your school doesn't have such access to tutoring you can purchase services directly from the vendor. These external tutoring services provide support with general science, math, and English courses. Both vendors offer specific support for nursing courses. These are good value for those needing additional assistance.

When studying your notes, attempt to understand the rationale for the information being presented. This will help you gain a greater understanding of the material. It's impossible to memorize the content. Understanding the basic concepts, particularly physiology and pathophysiology, will allow you to rationally think through solutions to many questions.

Tips on Taking Nursing Examinations

A question on a nursing exam is typically created into three parts: 1) case or scenario which describes what is happening to the patient; 2) the stem where the question is asked; and 3) the distracters which are the incorrect or in some cases less correct answers. Critical thinking is required as you have to distinguish between the options to determine which is most important. This will guide you in answering the stem. All answers may be correct with one being the most correct.

Read all of the instructions carefully before beginning the exam. Carefully read each question so you clearly understand the stem and what is being asked. Obviously, only answer what is asked in the stem. It's very easy to read into the question and not focus on what is being asked. Logically think through the priorities of the response. If you're asked to respond to only one option than clearly identify which one is of the highest priority. Keep in mind some questions ask select all that apply, so read the question carefully.

Go back to Maslow's hierarchy of needs beginning with physiology, basic safety, and so forth. The ABC of resuscitation (airway, breathing, and circulation) can also be helpful when prioritizing the answers and using the nursing process of assessment, planning, implementing, and evaluating may be useful. Psychosocial issues are typically focused on the individual in helping them to understand what they are asking. The correct responses are typically reflective in nature.

Keep track of the time you have to complete the exam. Thus pacing yourself is critical. Make sure that you answer all of the questions on the examination. Ensure that you place your responses on the bubble sheet (if such is being used) at the time that you answer the question. Do not wait and go back to put in the answers on the bubble sheet as this may mean you to not finish in time.

Keywords in the stem should guide you in selecting the correct answer or answers. Use caution when selecting answers that limit or qualify a potentially correct answer. Understand the keywords as it relates to the patient. Clues regarding the patient that may be critical for you to think about are age, gender, race, religion, and marital status. Identify what are the issue(s) being asked. Could it be a specific disease, a psychosocial issue, etc.?

A good approach would be to answer the question in your head prior to reading the possible options. Ensure you read all of the choices before making a final selection. It is good to use a process of elimination as one of your initial steps. Often the response comes down to a choice between two different ones. Logically think through the answers as they are presented and determine the prioritization of care based on those answers, remembering that one is more correct than another. In those questions where you are not sure of the correct answer start by eliminating the incorrect options. Then when all else fails guess.

Study Groups

If you are the type of person who benefits from interacting with others, than participating in a study group is probably a great option. Limit the study group to 4-5 classmates. Set up the written ground rules in how the group is going to function. For example, the ground rules should include: how the agenda/topics for the study group are going to be decided; how frequently will the group meet; the location of the meeting; how long is each session going to be; attendance/commitment expectations including being on time and prepared for each session; and who is going to be the gatekeeper to insure the meetings are focused. Remember creating a group takes trust, commitment, and mutual respect for each other. Your first attempt may not work because finding the right mix of people may take time.

Test Anxiety

Nursing students seem to have a high propensity for test anxiety than a number of other students. In a study of 600 undergraduate nursing students, Driscoll, R., G. Evans, G. Ramsey, S. Wheeler (2009) found 35% had test anxiety. The cause is not known; however, given the critical importance of nursing decisions on potentially the life and death of patients', it is hypothesized students may transfer this concern to their examinations.

Some anxiety can be helpful; however, to much can interfere with your ability to study and retain the information as well as your ability to take an exam by hindering your recall.

To determine if you may have test anxiety the *Westside Test Anxiety Scale* is an instrument to assist you with determining such. This assessment can be completed on line at Westside Test Anxiety Scale In some severe situations anxiety may be a medical diagnosis for which the student can request disability assistance.

Suggestions for management of anxiety can be found at this anxiety self help site. Anxiety Self Help Other options are to seek professional assistance through your college's counseling services or local professionals.

Classroom Tips

Be on time to class - arriving early, taking your seat, getting your notepad and pen ready, and focusing your mind on the situation will markedly enhance your ability to retain the material that is taught

Take notes - place a special emphasis on those topics that the faculty member emphasizes. Keep in mind however, some faculty has special interest in certain topics and may spend more time discussing them then is necessary to be successful on the NCLEX® examination. Thus, it's critical that you link your notes to the course objectives and topics being discussed that particular week to ensure you are gaining the essential knowledge needed to understand the material being taught.

Ask questions - engaging the faculty member with your questions is a critical component in developing your critical thinking and application skills. Take advantage of your expert faculty member to help clarify concepts, case study questions, and so forth. It is very important you thoroughly understand the material.

Participate in a study group - working with three or four others who have the same level of motivation to excel can markedly enhance your success. As a team, you may decide to break out the course material into different sections and review such with each other prior to class and perhaps most importantly as a team work together to prepare for the examination. Each person will bring a different skill set to the small group and you can learn from one another. Peer to peer learning is a critical ingredient to your success in nursing school.

Absolutely do not work during the school week - the number one way to fail in the nursing program is to spend too many hours working particularly during the week when you are participating in classroom lectures and while in clinical practice. If you must work, limit such time to the weekend. Recall earlier the discussion regarding the importance of arranging your financials so you can devote your time to school. The number one reason for failure of students is attempting to work and attend nursing school. Nursing school is very difficult in fact many say more challenging than medical school. Thus attempting to work excessively and balance the rest of your life and go to school full-time is not going to work for most people.

Complete at least 50 NCLEX® questions weekly with 90% accuracy - religiously following this prescription will ensure your exposure to a vast amount of content. It is necessary to be successful on NCLEX® test plan that these practice questions are completed.

Limit the amount of caffeine and other stimulants - too much caffeine will eventually lead to poor concentration and retention of the material.

Managing stress is critical - nursing school in itself is very stressful and when combined with family and other obligations it can become even more worrisome. It's critical that you learn some meditation techniques that can be practice 10 minutes a day to help focus your anxiety and to create a positive imagery of your success. Another technique for stress management is exercise particularly walking or jogging. Writing down the stressors in a log may also be useful as this will allow some further reflections on them. These activities do not have to take a significant amount of time. It is important that you take time to reflect and not allow the stress to interfere with your wellbeing. A good test to determine how much stress you may be experiencing is if you find yourself waking up at night and not able to go back to sleep. While awake if your mind is racing with multiple thoughts about things that you've got to do and things you need to manage etc. this is a good indicator of a high stress level.

Listen to your faculty - nurse faculty members have been in the practice arena for a number of years. They bring a wealth of knowledge and experience from the clinical setting into the classroom. You may not always agree with them and it is important that you learn from them by asking questions and listening to what they have to say.

Create a monthly calendar - the calendar should include time to study before each class, due dates for assignments, which benchmarks you need to achieve in order to finish on time, as well as balancing your work, family, and social events. Ensuring that you plan for your future at least 30 days out will enable you to be more successful in meeting your various obligations. Don't forget in your planning calendar to include time for studying, time for writing papers, and so forth.

CHAPTER SEVEN

Clinical Expectations

The heart of nursing is in clinical practice. The didactic material provides you the knowledge and competencies needed to use the nursing process to provide care to patients. The clinical arena is where you will gain expertise in clinical practice. Your faculty supervises all student nursing clinical activities.

All boards of nursing have regulations related to clinical simulation. Some states are very prescriptive such as Colorado that required 750 hours of clinical practice. Other states while not making specific clock hour requirement indicates in their regulations the need for adequate clinical practice to insure students are safe entry-level practitioners.

In nursing school you will have clinical practice in typically three different modules of learning all supervised by your faculty. They are in the skills lab, simulation, will and in actual practice with real patients.

Skills Laboratory

Your supply kit will supplement what you will find in the laboratory as you become proficient in performing a variety of clinical skills. Most schools of nursing have a clinical skills competency list of essentials that the student must demonstrate proficiency prior to graduation. The skills range from basic hygiene care of patients, making a bed (including when the patient is in it), bathing a patient who is bedridden, feeding a patient, getting the patient out of bed, providing oral care, administering an enema, etc. More complex competencies includes:

Putting on sterile gloves and gowning

Maintaining a sterile field

Drawing blood

Taking blood cultures

Taking vital signs (pulses, blood pressure, pain assessment, and temperature)

Measuring glucose levels

Administration of medications through various routes (such as topical, intradermal, intramuscular, and subcutaneous)

How to mix and administer insulin

Starting an intravenous (IV) line for the administration of medication including the use of an infusion pump

Peripherally inserted central catheter (PICC) care and changing including removing such

Changing dressings (including sterile dressings)

Changing colostomy bags while maintaining skin care

Chest tubes

Inserting indwelling Foley catheters

Inserting nasal gastric (NG) tube insertions and proper placement

Enteral feedings

Total perenteral nutrition (TPN) feeding

Sterile suctioning such as for tracheostomy

Attaching electrocardiograms (EKG) leads and reading EKG strips and monitors

Leopold maneuvers (used when caring for pregnant patients

In the skills laboratory you will have amble opportunities to become competent in these and other essential skills. In addition, the integration of the nursing process in the management of patients will also incur in the simulation laboratory and lastly in the actual care of patients.

Please keep in mind for practical nurses the skills list will vary given the scope of practice is different than for registered nurses. Your fundamental course textbook will provide detail information regarding the various skill competencies you will need to master. As you progress in the nursing curriculum, additional skills may be added and of course increase practice is critical.

The skills laboratory will have DVDs on all of the major procedures so you can also have a visual demonstration of most of the skills. There will also be simulated arms for practice in starting IVs, mannequins for inserting NG tubes, indwelling Foley catheters, to name the most common. There will also be hospitals beds for practice, wheel chairs, and linen to learn how to make a bed, crutches and canes, oxygen administration and suction devises.

In addition, to the lab time with your clinical instructor there will also be adequate time for you to practice these various competencies. In most programs there will be a skills check off so your ability to safely perform the various activities will be assessed. They are generally graded on a pass/fail basis. Bottom line you need to keep the skills check off list with you when in the clinical settings. The goal is for you to become as competent as possible in performing these tasks with real patients.

Simulation

Most schools of nursing also have simulation units in addition to the skills laboratory. Human patient simulation has become a common teaching method to provide more realistic clinical practice. These high fidelity mannequins using the latest innovations are programmed to react much the same as a real patient. Students are provided opportunities to practice with these "simulated virtual patients" to learn how to use the nursing process in managing various patient conditions without placing real humans at risk. Students can practice their ability to assess, plan, intervene and evaluate their care of patients with a variety of health dysfunctions. The simulations learning activities need to be related to the planned objectives in a realistic patient scenario that is directed by an experienced faculty member. The simulation activity needs to include a debriefing and evaluation of the student's performance. Simulation is not a substitute for faculty supervised patient care; rather a teaching strategy to assist students in learning to provide safe, competent, and hands-on practice.

There are a number of *YouTube* postings that demonstrate the use of simulation in nursing. An overview of simulation can be found at *Memorial Health Simulation Center* Memorial Health Simulation Center while specific use of simulation in managing patients can be found at Case Study in Managing a Trauma Patient Using Simulation which shows how to manage a trauma patient.

The *National League for Nursing's Simulation Innovation Resource Center* is an excellent site to learn about simulation in nursing practice. The National League of Nursing in collaboration with others, is in the final stages of an evaluation of simulation in nursing education. The site can be found at http://sirc.nln.org

Most state boards of nursing allow some of the required clinical practice to be done via simulation. The average is 25% with Texas allowing up to 50% simulation. On the other hand, New York does not allow any simulation experiences to be counted for required clinical time. The simulation needs to be clearly linked to the student learning outcomes and course objectives. Students should have an opportunity to evaluate simulation to insure, from their perspective, they are benefiting from such.

Clinical Practice with Real Patients
The skills laboratory and simulation provides you the exposure to the essential clinical competencies you will need to provide nursing care to real patients. Each medical/surgical, maternity and child health, psychiatric mental health and community health course have clinical practice components. As previously indicated part of the

practice may be completed in the skills laboratory, simulation center or a combination of such.

The clinical agency as mentioned previously requires you have the necessary immunizations, have been screened for a criminal background, have a current CPR card, and have completed an agency orientation specifically for nursing students. Your faculty member with the exception of the capstone course where RN preceptors may be used (depends on the curriculum model and State Board of Nursing regulations) is required to be at the clinical site with the students. Each state and some clinical agencies have rules regarding how many students one faculty member may supervise at one time. The rules typically range between 8 -10 students per faculty.

Students are expected to adhere to standards of conduct as specified in the school of nursing student handbook when in the clinical settings. This includes an approved uniform with a nametag, personal appearance, complying with a drug free environment, patient confidentially rules, and professional communication. In addition, students need to have a pen, small note pad, ideally a smart phone pre-load with reference material, and any required documentation regarding your assigned patient(s). *Keep in mind some clinical agencies may not allow the use of smart phones thus reference books need to be a part of your backup plan.

Depending on the course and protocol at the clinical agency or school students may visit the clinical site the night prior to clinical to identify a patient for which he/she will provide nursing care for the following day. The student will take basic information from the chart regarding the patient and then secure from the patient(s) permission to care for him/her the next day. A log is maintained at the clinical unit so nurses know which patients have been selected. The student is responsible for being prepared to address the nursing needs of the patient, medications, laboratory values, and treatments with the instructor the next day. For beginning students the faculty member typically selects the patient in advance.

Generally students are NOT allowed to administer any medications unless the faculty member is physically present with the student at the time of administration. The same protocol is also used in regards to performing any treatments or clinical procedures. Your faculty member will orally quiz you about your assigned patient. Particular focus will be on the patients medical diagnosis, pathophysiology of the diseases present, nursing process related questions, and medications. The medications will be a particular focus with insuring you understand the rationale for their use, typical dosage, and side effects. There may also be a need to have some other written documentation you have prepared regarding your patient. If allowed this is a great time to have your smart phone as you can quickly look up information regarding your patient's condition, medications, and any procedures needed.

Another important component of your clinical practice will be documenting your assessments and care provided to your patients. With the requirement for electronic health records, it is likely your documentation will be done electronically. In most cases your faculty member will ask you to write out your entry prior to it being entered into the permanent electronic record. In some cases the note may still be hand written onto a paper chart.

In most cases you must be at the clinical site ahead of the time scheduled. Most programs have strict rules regarding being late for clinical as well as uniform and personal appearance requirements. Most programs have a mechanism for addressing clinical absence. Some charge for clinical make-ups and all have a maximum number of clinical hours that can be missed.

Some capstone courses (the last course in your degree plan) may use a preceptor model. In this teaching model the student works one-on-one with the nursing staff member. The nurse is the student's preceptor working along side him/her. The student works the same shift as the preceptor. This model allows the student to gain increasing independence in caring for more complex groups of patients as would be expected of an entry level nurse. The faculty member monitors the student's performance in collaboration with the preceptor.

Your instructor evaluates your clinical performance including students matched with a preceptor. The instructor assesses your ability to meet the specific clinical objectives identified for the course. The instructor provides a midterm evaluation and your final assessment. You will be asked to verify the evaluation by signing the clinical evaluation form. The grade in most cases is pass/fail. The instructor will ask the preceptor nursing staff to participate in your evaluation. However, the faculty member is ultimately responsible for your final grade.

In a rare situation in which the student demonstrates unsafe practice, unprofessional conduct and/or does not improve with faculty coaching he/she may be immediately removed from the clinical site and given a failure for the clinical component of the course. Patient safely is the ultimate guideline. There can be no short cut related to insuring no harm comes to the patient for which students are providing nursing care. A failure in a clinical component is also considered a failure in the didactic portion of the course.

CHAPTER EIGHT

Program Evaluation

All nursing programs must have a plan for systematic evaluation of its program. As a student you will be asked to participate in at least three types of evaluations: 1) course(s) at the end of academic term; 2) end of program; and 3) around six months after graduation an alumni survey.

The course evaluations will be administered during the last week of the term. The questions will be related to your opinion about the quality of the course related to your learning needs as well as an opportunity to provide feedback regarding your instructor. These evaluations are anonymous and your response cannot be identified. Some schools may have the evaluations completed online while others use a paper and pencil response using a bubble answer sheet.

The end of program evaluation is given to graduating students. This assessment will ask you to evaluate to what degree you met the student learning outcomes for your particular degree. There will also be questions about satisfaction with support services such as financial aid, academic advising, and other student support services. Questions related to satisfaction with the tuition and fees charged for the degree, overall quality of the education, and if you would recommend the program to others are generally asked.

The alumni survey is the last general assessment you will be asked to complete. This survey is typically mailed or a link to a web page sent via email about six months after graduation. This survey is similar to the end of program survey with a greater focus on your assessment how you think six months after graduation about your ability to meet the student learning outcomes. In addition, questions regarding your overall satisfaction and if you would refer a friend to the program may be asked.

Please note the exact questions on any of these forms will vary by school and in some cases accreditation requirements. Academic administers carefully review all evaluations to assess students' perceptions and satisfaction with the faculty member. The school's curriculum and evaluation committees will also review your assessments. The data will be used for reports to regulatory and accrediting agencies. The school will then use the feedback for improvement as necessary. Faculty will also receive a copy of his/her individual evaluations

CHAPTER NINE

Extracurricular Activities

In nursing school you will have an opportunity to participate in a variety of extracurricular activities. It is strongly suggested that you engage in such activities as it will provide you a richer personal and academic experience. In addition, when it comes time for interviews with prospective employers, you can demonstrate that you were also engaged in a variety of activities outside of your academic studies.

Student Nurses Association

Many schools have a chapter of the student nurses association. These school chapters are a part of a larger state chapter which in turn is a part of the National Student Nurses Association. The National Student Nurses Association (NSNA) reports a membership of over 60,000. This organization is for students in registered nurse pre-licensure programs. They have a variety of outreach activities, resources, and scholarship programs. Their website can be found at National Student Nurses Association This organization and affiliates provides students the opportunity to become involved in professional organizations and activities.

School Advisory Council

Most nursing programs have a student Council which is chartered to provide students a voice in the governance of the school. Generally they have bylaws which guide their activities. Each cohort of students elects their representatives to attend the organizing group for the school. This provides a forum for students to have input into school governance issues. In some cases, representatives from the Council serve on curriculum, evaluation, and other committees. Students will have an opportunity to meet with faculty in these various committees as well as the nursing academic administration. Student input into the overall governance of the program is welcomed and valued.

Study Abroad

The opportunity to participate in international study abroad programs may also be available in your school. These programs are typically sponsored by the College and/or school and allow you to have an opportunity to visit a different country. Learning activities are generally health related and provide the student an opportunity for not only a cultural exchange but perhaps to provide nursing care in an international setting.

The structure of these programs varies depending on the purpose of the study abroad. In some cases students participate as a part of a nonprofit health related organization international outreach. Other times the activity may be arranged by the school of nursing working in collaboration with a school of nursing in another country. For the latter activity you may be able to achieve course credit. If you have an opportunity to participate in one of these events it is recommended that you do so.

Community Service Projects

A number of colleges provide an opportunity for students to be engaged in a variety of community service projects. Typically in nursing school this may be participating in a health fair, a walk for breast cancer research, food drive for the homeless, etc. The student nurses association, in many cases, is the driver of these activities. It's a very enriching experience for students to participate in these events. Learning to give back to your fellow citizens is an important role modeling behavior the schools like to foster with their students.

CHAPTER TEN

Afterword

Nursing is both an art and science. The blending of the two is central to your future success as a nurse. The science provides the scientific foundation for your practice and the art is the humanistic touch and the intuitive sense of knowing when to apply the science. Nursing is unique as most nurses choose the profession because of his/her desire to care for others.

Jean Watson (2012), a nurse who is best known for her theory of caring, states: "Caring is a science that encompasses a humanitarian, human science orientation, human care processes, phenomena, and experiences". Caring is transpersonal as it acknowledges life and connections that move back and forth from individual, others, community, nation, world, and eventually the universe. According to Watson, the goal is to help the patient gain a higher degree of harmony with mind, body, and soul. This is done through caring which encompasses the science of nursing. The patient is viewed as a biological, psychological, social, and spiritual being. As nurses we care for the entire person. This is a link to Dr. Watson's caring center: Watson Caring Science Institute

Some postulate that perhaps at some point in nursing an admission requirement might be an assessment of the applicant's ability to use his/her life force to assist others with their will to get better or to make their transition out of this life. Thus as a student entering nursing you are beginning a journey that will be life transforming for you and others around you. Perhaps most importantly will be the use of your caring ability when integrating the art and science of the practice of nursing.

Good Karma on your journey!!

I would like to thank my life partner Daniel Jaramillo of 30 plus years for his unconditional love and support. He provides ongoing support and encouragement for me. In particular, I also want to thank all of the military colleagues I have had the pleasure to serve with, nursing students, faculty, academic administrators, and nurses with whom I have worked during my 40 plus years as a registered nurse. To Dr. Rosanna Harrigan a special thank you. She continues to be my mentor and biggest supporter particularly in my career as an academic administrator. These individuals provided the inspiration for this book. A special thanks to Jim Flahive, RN, MSN and Yvette Bowman, RN, MSN for their critical review of the manuscript. An additional thank you to Alex Rodriguez, recent nursing graduate who read the manuscript and made invaluable comments to insure the content was designed to assist new nursing students with their transition to nursing school. I thank them all.

Robert L Anders was born in Delta, Colorado in 1947. He is a registered nurse and a retired lieutenant colonel in the United States Army having served 24 years as a Nurse Corp officer. He has received numerous military and civilian honors including being inducted as a Fellow in the American Academy of Nursing and a Fellow in the National League of Nursing Academy of Nursing Education. He has numerous publications including a book co-author with Dr. James Hawkins *Mosby's Nursing Leadership and Management Online*. In addition, Dr. Anders is a funded researcher and educator by a variety of Federal, State, and private agencies. He is an expert in minority health disparities and in educating socially and economic disadvantaged nurses. Dr. Anders has held a variety of academic and educational leadership positions. He lives in El Paso, Texas and enjoys spending summers in Pea Green, Colorado, his boyhood home.

Beck, A. (1997). The past and future of cognitive therapy. *Journal of psychotherapy practice and research, 6*(4). 276-286.

Driscoll, R., G. Evans, G. Ramsey, S. Wheeler (2009). High Test Anxiety among Nursing Students. *ERIC*, 3pp

Ellis, A. (1973). Humanistic psychotherapy: the rational emotive approach. New York: Julian Press.

Frith, K, Sewell, J.P,, & Clark, D.J. (November/December, 2005). Best practices in NCLEX-RN Readiness preparation for baccalaureate student success. Computers, Informatics, Nursing, 23(6), p. 322-329.

(McDowell, 2007; Firth, Sewell, & Clark, 2005; McQueen, Shelton, & Zimmerman, 2004; Stark, Feikema, Wyngarten, 2002; Williams & Bryant, 2001).

McQueen, L., Shelton, P., & Zimmermann, L. (2004). A collective community approach to preparing nursing students for the NCLEX-RN examination, AGNF Journal, 15, 55-68.

Stark, M.A., Feikema, B., & Wyngarden, K. (2002). Empowering students for NCLEX success: Self-assessment and planning. Nurse Educator, 27, 103-105.

Test Success: A Module for . Retrieved from the Internet on November 13, 2012 at Test Success

Watson, Jean (2012). Watson Caring Science Institute: International Carita Consortium. Retrieved from the Internet on November 13, 2012 at http://www.watsoncaringscience.org/index.cfm

Williams, D., & Bryant, S. (2001). Preparing at-risk baccalaureate students for NCLEX success. Kentucky Nurse, 49(1), 17.